HOW TO RAISE AND TRAIN AN

Irish Setter

by Robert Gannon

Distributed in the U.S.A. by T.F.H. Publications, Inc., 211 West Sylvania Avenue, P.O. Box 27, Neptune City, N.J. 07753; in England by T.F.H. (Gt. Britain) Ltd., 13 Nutley Lane, Reigate, Surrey; in Canada to the book store and library trade by Clarke, Irwin & Company, Clarwin House, 791 St. Clair Avenue West, Toronto 10, Ontario; in Canada to the pet trade by Rolf C. Hagen Ltd., 3225 Sartelon Street, Montreal 382, Quebec; in Southeast Asia by Y.W. Ong, 9 Lorong 36 Geylang, Singapore 14; in Australia and the south Pacific by Pet Imports Pty. Ltd., P.O. Box 149, Brookvale 2100, N.S.W., Australia. Published by T.F.H. Publications, Inc. Ltd., The British Crown Crown Colony of Hong Kong.

Photos by Louise Van der Meid with the cooperation of
Mr. & Mrs. Tom Palmer, Mr. & Mrs. Padrick and their
daughter, Sybil Webb, Maurice Heise, Mrs. Lillian
Carson, Christie Cummins and Bill Evans.

ISBN 0-87666-319-6

Manufactured in the United States of America
Library of Congress Catalog Card No.: 60-14333

Contents

Your regal Irish Setter is an aristocrat. He is dignified and intelligent, always well-mannered, even with strangers. Yet while he is a perfect companion for the home, he is also excellent in woods and field.

1. History of the Breed

Once an Irish Setter has been pointed out to you, you'll never forget what the breed looks like. Among all the breeds recognized as pure, only the Irish Setter is the color of solid mahogany, or, as someone once said, "the russet of a freshly opened horse chestnut burr."

Irish Setters are not only handsome, poised dogs, they are also wonderful companions. They are good hunting partners for men, reliable household protectors for women, and even-tempered rough-and-tumble playmates for children. They are long-lived, gentle and affectionate, and they never yap or howl. Even with strangers, they have perfect manners. Well aware of their size, they never knock over young children or furniture. They are intelligent enough to know their place, both around the house and in the field.

Setters belong to the group known as Sporting Dogs, a group used primarily for hunting birds. This group also includes the Pointers, Spaniels and Retrievers. Like all Sporting Dogs, Setters are good-looking, hardy and highly intelligent. In addition to the Irish, the American Kennel Club recognizes two other Setters—the English and the Gordon. The Irish Setter is currently the most popular of the three in the United States.

THE IRISH SETTER'S BACKGROUND

Little is known about the early development of the Irish Setter, mainly because those who were responsible for the early breedings were more interested in results than in keeping records. The only thing genealogists agree upon is that there is a great deal of Spaniel blood in the Irish Setter. There are many different kinds of Spaniels, though, and exactly what Spaniel blood is open to question. Early writings on the subject claim the French, Italian, Spanish and Irish Water Spaniel as forefathers of the Irish Setter.

Together with the Spaniels, a number of other breeds were also the ancestors of today's Irish Setter. Among them were the Bloodhound—a strain that shows in the pendulous ears, throatiness and prominent occiput (back part of the head) of some Irish Setters. Pointer blood also shows in the short coat, pronounced stop and lean toward "roach" back that occasionally appears in Irish Setters. The Gordon Setter may also have played a part, as indicated by black puppies in some litters of Irish Setters. Some people also say that the English Setter was crossbred with the Irish Setter early in the breed's history.

At any rate the development from Spaniel to Setter took a good many years, during which the words "Spaniel" and "Setter" were apparently used interchangeably. In certain 14th-century paintings, dogs that look to us like Spaniels are labeled Setters. Yet in 1685 John Harris of County Worcester, England, signed a contract in which he agreed to "fully and effectually traine up and teach a Spanill named Quaud to Sitt Partridges, Pheasants and other game, as well and exactly as the best sitting Dogges usually sett the same." The contract uses the word "Spaniel" but it describes the duties of a dog that we would call a Setter. The name "Setter" comes from the word "set." Before firearms came into widespread use, Setters actually "set" or stopped game, principally partridge, so the hunter could trap the birds in a large net.

Sometime around 1750 the term "Setting Spaniel" came into use. This was about the time when hunters began using guns. The first firearms for hunting birds were huge assemblies with large bores and with barrels 5 or 6 feet long. Hunters used guns mainly on water birds and continued to use nets for land fowl. When the flintlock came into use and guns became somewhat more portable and common, hunters needed a dog with longer legs than the Spaniel. Since the gun enabled the hunter to kill his prey more quickly and from a greater distance, his dog had to be able to run faster and farther. Thus, Pointers and Setters became popular.

Setters from Ireland started to develop characteristics of their own, and gradually three distinct color strains emerged—red and white combined, red with tiny white dots, and solid red. In time the solid red color became the accepted color for all Irish Setters.

Proof that Irish Setter owners valued their dogs highly is that a selling price of 100 guineas (equal to about $300) was not unheard of around 1800, when $300 was a good deal more money than it is now.

Throughout the history of the breed, Pointers have been crossbred with Irish Setters. According to historians, this has been responsible for the great number of what doggy people call "droppers" or unregistered dogs. In some cases these crossbreeds have turned out to be splendid gun dogs, but in most cases they emphasize the poor points of both breeds and lack the outstanding traits of either one.

In 1860 the first show with a separate Irish Setter division was held at Birmingham, England. For the most part the Irish Setters were still red and white combined. The first indication of the trend toward solid red dogs came 15 years later at a Dublin show, where out of 66 Irish Setters entered, 43 were solid red.

In the meantime, the Irish Setter was being imported in large numbers to the United States. The first Irish Setter to become an outstanding show dog in America was a dog named Elcho, imported in 1875. He distinguished himself both in the field and on the bench at dog shows.

In later years, however, Setters, especially Irish, lost out in field trials to the Pointers. The reason was that Irish Setter owners had become so proud of the looks of their dogs that they thought only of the bench and slackened off on breeding for the field.

Recently, though, there has been a turn toward breeding and training for the field also, so that Irish Setters have become more of an all-round dog, much to the pleasure of Irish Setter owners.

The Irish is gentle, particularly with tiny children. This dog seems to understand that his size may make children a little frightened at first and he makes up for this by being extremely docile and patient.

PERSONALITY

A striking reflection of the isle that bred him, the Irish Setter has more fire than the English and is a shade more rambunctious than the Gordon. Still, he is gentle, affectionate and never bad-tempered unless provoked to the extreme. His amiable disposition makes him a perfect playmate for children, and his tough hide and impressive bulk make him sturdier than most of the smaller breeds.

It has been said (always by owners of other breeds) that the Irish is the slowest learner among the Setters. Perhaps this is so, but equally important, he is a slow forgetter. He may need a bit more training in the field, to learn not to pounce on a waiting bird, for instance, but once he does learn, he's a dog that knows his role for the rest of his life.

The Irish Setter is a dog with plenty of endurance. When the day's hunting is through, when after wading through ice-cold swamps, crawling through bramble patches and plowing through waist-high snow, you're ready to drop from exhaustion, your Setter will still be raring to go, wondering why you called a halt.

All in all, when you own a well-trained Irish Setter, whether he is a dog for the field, for showing or merely a companionable friend, you've got yourself a real dog—one whose faithfulness, mild disposition, intelligence and beauty will ensure your continuing pride.

STANDARDS OF THE BREED

The standards which have been adopted by the Irish Setter Club of America and approved by the American Kennel Club set the present-day ideal for which

"What am I doing in this getup!" Whether dressed for bed or for a circus ring, this Setter seems mortified by his costume. Although Setters do not particularly enjoy clowning, they are not easily irritated by the antics of human beings trying to get them to perform.

Irish Setter breeders are aiming. It is by these standards that the dog is judged in the show ring. However, even the most perfect specimen falls short of the standards in some respect. It's also impossible, even for a breeder or veterinarian, to tell how a puppy will shape up as an adult dog. The chances are that he will inherit the qualities for which his father and mother—or sire and dam in dog language—were bred, and if both his parents and grandparents had good show records he may have excellent possibilities.

Here, then, are the standards.

HEAD: Should be long and lean. The skull oval (from ear to ear) having plenty of brain room and with well-defined occipital protuberance. Brows raised, showing stop. The muzzle moderately deep and fairly square at end. From the stop to the point of the nose should be long, the nostrils wide and the jaws of nearly equal length, flews not to be pendulous. The color of the nose dark mahogany or dark chocolate and that of the eyes (which ought not to be too large) rich hazel or brown. The ears to be of moderate size, fine in texture, set on low, well back and hanging in a neat fold close to the head.

NECK: Should be moderately long, very muscular but not too thick, slightly arched, free from all tendency to throatiness.

BODY: Should be proportionately long, shoulders fine at the points, deep and sloping well back. The chest deep, rather narrow in front. The ribs well sprung, leaving plenty of lung room. The loins muscular and slightly arched. The hindquarters wide and powerful.

LEGS AND FEET: The hind legs from hip to hock should be long and muscular, from hock to heel short and strong. The stifle and hock joints well bent, and not inclined either in or out. The forelegs should be strong and sinewy, having plenty of bone, with elbows free, well let down and like the hock not inclined either out or in. The feet rather small, very firm, toes strong, close together and arched.

TAIL: Should be of moderate length, set on rather low, strong at root and tapering to a fine point; to be carried in a slight scimitar-like curve or straight, nearly level with the back.

COAT: On the head, front of legs and tips of ears should be short and fine, but on all other parts of the body it should be of moderate length, flat and as free as possible from curl or wave.

FEATHERING: The feather on the upper portion of the ears should be long and silky, on the back of forelegs and hind legs long and fine, a fair amount of hair on belly, forming a nice fringe, which may extend on chest and throat. Feet to be well feathered between the toes. Tail to have a nice fringe of moderately long hair, decreasing in length as it approaches the point. All feathering to be as straight and as flat as possible.

COLOR AND MARKINGS: The color should be a rich golden chestnut or mahogany red, with no trace whatever of black; white on chest, throat or toes, or a small star on forehead, or a narrow streak, or blaze on the nose or face not to disqualify.

JUDGING POINTS

When comparing Irish Setters in the show ring, the judges rate them on the following scale of points.

Head	10
Eyes	5
Ears	5
Neck	5
Body	15
Shoulders, forelegs and feet	12
Hind legs	10
Tail	8
Coat and feather	8
Color	8
Size, style and general appearance	14
Total	100

2. Selecting Your Irish Setter

Puppies of any breed are cute and irresistible, but puppies don't stay tiny and helpless for long. The full-grown Irish Setter stands about 2 feet tall, weighs up to about 75 pounds and requires about 1½ pounds of food a day. Irish Setters are more active than the other Setters and need plenty of exercise. With exceptional care they can be kept in city apartments, but this necessitates long walks—a mile or two a day—if the dogs are to be kept in first-class shape.

Once you decide that the Irish Setter is the dog for you, how do you go about choosing the right one, when you are faced with a group of Irish puppies at the kennels? Your first interest should be in obtaining a healthy animal. Try to select the one that's the most active and aggressive. If the puppies have just been fed and are sleepy, wait a while before making your selection. Check the dog's eyes and ears for any puslike discharge, and pass him over if his eyes or ears are running. A running nose or a very dry nose can also be a danger sign in a young puppy. Look at his teeth and gums and make sure they are not bleeding. If the puppy is having a bowel movement, it should not be watery.

Avoid a puppy that is thick-set, that has bow legs, a flat skull or large, widely-set eyes. You can't tell much about the dog's ultimate color, but if the puppy's coat is very light or dead-looking, or if there are bare spots, better pass him up. As you look the puppies over, compare them as well as you can with the ideal adult dog described in the standard.

It is always wise to make your purchase subject to the approval of a veterinarian. The seller will usually allow you eight hours in which to take the puppy to a vet to have his health checked. Arrive at a clear agreement with the seller on what happens if the vet rejects the puppy. It should be understood whether rejection means you get your money back or merely the choice of another puppy.

All purebred puppies should have an American Kennel Club registration and a pedigree for at least three generations. Ask to see copies of these, and look for the "Ch." in the listings of the dog's parents and grandparents. This denotes dogs that have won their breed championships.

MALE OR FEMALE?

If you should intend breeding your dog in the future, by all means buy a female. You can find a suitable mate without difficulty when the time comes, and have the pleasure of raising a litter of pups—there is nothing cuter than a fat, playful puppy. If you don't want to raise puppies, your female can be spayed, and will remain a healthy, lively pet. The female is smaller than the male and generally quieter. She has less tendency to roam in search of ro-

"Me! Please take me home!" Choosing among these appealing little fellows is a heart-breaking job, but there is no doubt about it; eventually they will all have homes.

mance, but a properly trained male can be a charming pet, and has a certain difference in temperament that is appealing to many people. Male vs. female is chiefly a matter of personal choice.

ADULT OR PUP?

Whether to buy a grown dog or a small puppy is another question. It is undeniably fun to watch your dog grow all the way from a baby, sprawling and playful, to a mature, dignified dog. If you don't have the time to spend on the more frequent meals, housebreaking, and other training a puppy needs in order to become a dog you can be proud of, then choose an older, partly trained pup or a grown dog. If you want a show dog, remember that no one, not even an expert, can predict with 100 per cent accuracy what a small puppy will be when he grows up. If you're looking for a dog that is trained for hunting, ask if you can take him out for a trial run. If the seller refuses for no good reason, better think twice about buying his dog.

HOW TO REGISTER YOUR IRISH SETTER

As a rule, the puppy you buy has not been registered as an individual, but the breeder has probably registered the litter. Unless he has done this, you cannot register your puppy with the American Kennel Club. Both the puppy's parents must have been registered as purebred Irish Setters too. An unregistered dog cannot qualify for dog show awards or for obedience degrees and its offspring will be less valuable.

To register with the A.K.C., obtain an Application for Registration from the seller who will fill in the lines on the form that transfer ownership to you. The form should also bear the signature of the owner of the dam (mother in dog-language). Then you select a name for your dog (it must be 25 letters or

These pups are curious and alert. Like all babies, they want to know what's going on around them and have popped up in their box to get a good look at the world outside.

less, and cannot duplicate the name of another dog of the breed, or be the name of a living person without his written permission). Enter the selected name on the form, fill in the blanks that make you the owner of record, and send it to the American Kennel Club, 221 Park Avenue South, New York, New York, with the required registration fee. In a few weeks you will receive a Certificate of Registration with your dog's name (if it is approved) and registration number.

Actually, all this isn't as complicated as it may appear. It's routine with the dog seller, and the forms are no more complicated than applications for a marriage license or a personal loan.

THE PEDIGREE

The pedigree of your dog is a tracing of his family tree. Often the breeder will have the pedigree of the dog's dam and sire and may make out a copy for you. Or, you can write to the American Kennel Club once your dog has been registered and ask for a pedigree. The fee depends on how many generations back you want the pedigree traced. In addition to giving the immediate ancestors of your dog, the pedigree will show whether there are any champions or dogs that have won obedience degrees in his lineage. If you are planning selective breeding, the pedigree is also helpful to enable you to find other Irish Setters that have the same general family background.

WORMING AND INOCULATION

Before you take your puppy home, find out from the breeder if he has already been wormed or inoculated for distemper and rabies. Practically all puppies will have worms, which they acquire from eating worm eggs, from fleas, or from their mother. The breeder usually gives the puppies a worming before he sells them. If yours has already been wormed, find out when and what treatment was given. The breeder may be able to advise you on any further treatment that is necessary. While there are many commercial worming preparations on the market, it's generally safer to let the vet handle it. There will be more about worms in Chapter 3.

If your puppy has been inoculated against distemper, you will also have to know when this was done so you can give the information to your vet. He will complete the series of shots. If your puppy has not yet been given this protection, your vet should take care of it immediately. Distemper is highly prevalent and contagious. Don't let your puppy out of doors until he has had his distemper shots and they have had time to take effect.

As a rule, kennels and breeders do not inoculate puppies against rabies. In some areas, rabies inoculation is required by law. However, the possibility of your dog's becoming affected with rabies, a contact disease, is very slight in most parts of the country. To be perfectly safe, check with your vet who will be familiar with the local ordinances and will advise you.

While the distemper inoculation is permanent and can be supplemented by "booster" shots, rabies inoculation must be repeated yearly. When your puppy receives it, the vet will give you a tag for the dog's collar certifying that he has received the protection. He will also give you a certificate for your own records. For foreign travel and some interstate travel, rabies inoculation is required.

Notice how confident this toddler is at the side of her Irish Setter. In spite of his elegant profile and silky coat, this breed is without vanity. The Irish is patient and reliable, a perfect companion for children.

3. Caring for Your Irish Setter

BRINGING YOUR PUPPY HOME

When you bring your puppy home, remember that he is used to the peace and relative calm of a life of sleeping, eating and playing with his brothers and sisters. The trip away from all this is an adventure in itself, and so is adapting to a new home. So let him take it easy for a while. Don't let the whole neighborhood pat and poke him at one time. Be particularly careful when children want to handle him, for they cannot understand the difference between the delicate living puppy and the toy dog they play with and maul. Show them the correct way to hold the puppy, supporting his belly with one hand while holding him securely with the other.

THE PUPPY'S BED

It is up to you to decide where the puppy will sleep. He should have his own place, and not be allowed to climb all over the furniture. He should sleep out of drafts, but not right next to the heat, which would make him too sensitive to the cold when he goes outside.

An Irish Setter puppy is a little too large to grow up in a box. You might partition off a section of a room—the kitchen is good because it's usually warm and he'll have some companionship there. Set up some sort of partition that he can't climb, give him a pillow or old blanket for his bed and cover the floor with a thick layer of newspapers.

Don't make the mistake of buying a bed or even a sleeping pad for a young puppy. He's certain to demolish it. You might buy some cedar shavings and make a "nest" of them. They help prevent a doggy odor and may discourage fleas.

You have already decided where the puppy will sleep before you bring him home. Let him stay there, or in the corner he will soon learn is "his," most of the time, so that he will gain a sense of security from the familiar. Give the puppy a little food when he arrives, but don't worry if he isn't hungry at first. He will soon develop an appetite when he grows accustomed to his surroundings. The first night the puppy may cry a bit from lonesomeness, but if he has an old blanket or rug to curl up in he will be cozy. In winter a hot water bottle will help replace the warmth of his littermates, or the ticking of a clock may provide company.

FEEDING THE PUPPY

The breeder or pet shop where you buy the puppy will tell you what he has been fed. It's a good idea to keep him on the same food for a while as a sudden change may cause an upset stomach.

These pups are enjoying one of their four daily meals. Perhaps the little fellow on the left looks sad because he knows he will not always be able to eat so often. After they are 4 or 5 months old, Setters are cut down to three and eventually, at 7 months, to two meals a day.

Until your puppy is 4 or 5 months old, feed him four times a day. In the morning give him some warm milk with a little cereal or egg added. Some veterinarians suggest a mashed hard-boiled egg with baby's cereal and a vitamin powder or liquid added. For the first few weeks the mixture should be about the consistency of a thick soup; later it can be even thicker. As to the amount, that depends on the rate at which your puppy is growing and how much activity he gets. If he leaves food, cut down the portions. If he laps up every bit and seems to want more, increase the amount.

At noontime, he should have a heavier meal. Use canned dog food, dog meal, kibbled food, ground beef or cooked horsemeat mixed with warm water, milk or broth. At about 5 P.M., give him a little more cereal and milk or some light dog food. At bedtime, give him a snack with less liquids. If you cut down the liquid later in the day, housebreaking will be easier. With so much liquid in his diet, your puppy probably won't drink much water. Try putting a dish of water in front of him during the day. If he doesn't want it, take it away or you'll have a damp puppy and a damp mess of papers to clean up.

After your puppy is 5 months old, you can begin to cut down on the morning and evening meals. By the time he is 7 months old, he should be on a two-meal-a-day routine, and at the age of 10 months to a year he should be content with one large meal and perhaps a snack in the morning and before bedtime.

Common sense is the most important factor in feeding a puppy or young dog. If your dog looks thin, he probably needs more food; if he is heavy after he outgrows his puppy fat, he may be overfed. If you find that some foods give him loose bowels or gas, change his menu. However, if you think you are feeding

This adult Setter seems to enjoy a loving hug, but puppies can't withstand much roughness. Children should be taught to handle their pets gently.

him properly and he isn't responding the way you think he should be, a trip to the vet might be advisable.

(For more detailed information on puppy feeding, see HOW TO RAISE AND TRAIN A PEDIGREED OR MIXED BREED PUPPY, another Sterling-T.F.H. book).

WATCHING THE PUPPY'S HEALTH

The first step in protecting the health of your puppy is a visit to the veterinarian. If the breeder has not given your puppy his first distemper shots, have your vet do it. You should also have your dog protected against hepatitis, and, if required by local law or if your vet suggests it, against rabies. Your puppy should receive his full quota of protective inoculations, especially if you plan to show him later. Select a veterinarian you feel you can trust and keep his phone number handy. Any vet will be glad to give a regular "patient" advice over the phone—often without charge.

Occasional loose bowels in a puppy generally isn't anything too serious. It can be the result of an upset stomach or a slight cold. Sometimes it will clear up in a day or so without any treatment. If you want to help the puppy's digestion, add some cottage cheese to his diet, or give him a few drops of kaopectate. Instead of tap water, give him barley or oatmeal water (just as you would a human baby). However, if the looseness persists for more than a day or two, a visit to the vet may be required. If the puppy has normal bowel movements alternating with loose bowel movements, it may be a symptom of worms.

If the puppy upchucks a meal or vomits up slime or white froth, it may indicate that his stomach is upset. One good stomach-settler is a pinch of baking soda, or about 8 or 10 drops of pure witch hazel in a teaspoon of cold water two or three times a day. In case of vomiting you should skip a few meals to give the stomach a chance to clear itself out. When you start to feed him again, give him cooked scraped beef for his first meals and then return to his normal diet. Persistent vomiting may indicate a serious stomach upset or even poisoning and calls for professional help.

SUGGESTED DIET FOR THE ADULT IRISH SETTER

An adult dog gets along best on one meal a day. You will probably find it most convenient to make this the evening meal and feed your dog at your own dinnertime. However, if you prefer, you can choose another time of the day, but it's best to have a regular schedule and feed your dog at about the same time every day.

The amount of food you give him depends on his activity. An active Irish Setter needs between 1 and $1\frac{1}{2}$ pounds of meat a day. Common sense is your best guide. If he rejects certain kinds of foods, don't try to force him to eat them. If you find that some foods upset his stomach, cut them out. The amount of flesh and fat on your dog's body is an indication of his diet's suitability. If he is overloaded with fat, it will show on the smooth-coated Irish Setter. On the other hand, if his ribs are too prominent and his hindquarters are gaunt, he may not be getting enough food or the right kind of food.

This is a well-fed Setter, as indicated by his coat and body. If he were being fed too much, his coat would reflect the results; if too little, his ribs would show and his hindquarters would be prominent and bony.

Your dog needs fat in his diet. If you are feeding him horsemeat or kibbled or other dry dog foods, add a handful of beef fat or some bacon drippings. Lack of fat will result in a poor coat or dull hair. The adult dog can use vitamins or cod-liver oil too.

If your dog skips an occasional meal, it is no cause for worry. If he isn't interested in eating, take the food away after 10 or 15 minutes. A number of kennels purposely eliminate one meal a week, feeling that it makes the dogs more active and alert. Many exhibitors do not feed their dogs the day of a show. Use your own judgment about that.

Whatever you do, don't pamper your dog as so many pet owners do. Remember that he has a stronger digestive system than you. His internal organs are like those of the fox and the wolf, and under natural conditions he would be eating raw meat without added vitamins or flavoring.

While he can eat almost everything you can, there are some foods you should avoid. A chicken or fish bone can lodge in his throat or cause intestinal trouble. Too many starches or too much sugar in his diet can affect his coat or upset his system since they are not natural foods for carnivorous animals. However, a piece of candy once in a while, a dish of ice cream or the leavings of a piece of pie won't harm him. When you're traveling, he can enjoy a hamburger or a hot dog as much as the other members of the family.

If your dog develops loose bowels but seems well otherwise, you can try a change of diet. If his meat has been served raw, try cooking it for a few days. Cottage cheese added to the diet often helps, as does barley or oatmeal water instead of plain tap water.

WORMING

Practically all puppies start out in life with worms in their insides, either acquired from the mother or picked up in their sleeping quarters. However, there are six different types of worms. Some will be visible in the stool as small white objects; others require microscopic examination of the stool for identification. While there are many commercial worm remedies on the market, it is safest to leave that to your veterinarian, and to follow his instructions on feeding the puppy before and after the worming. If you find that you must administer a worm remedy yourself, read the directions carefully and administer the smallest possible dose. Keep the puppy confined after treatment for worms, since many of the remedies have a strong laxative action and the puppy will soil the house if allowed to roam freely.

THE USEFUL THERMOMETER

Almost every serious puppy ailment shows itself by an increase in the puppy's body temperature. If your Irish Setter acts lifeless, looks dull-eyed and gives an impression of illness, check by using a rectal thermometer. Hold the dog, insert the thermometer which has been lubricated with vaseline and take a reading. The normal temperature is 100.6 to 101.5 (higher than the normal human temperature). Excitement may send it up slightly, but any rise of more than a few points is cause for alarm.

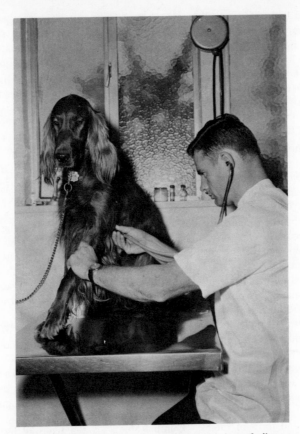

His listless expression shows that this Irish Setter is not feeling up
to par. At a time like this the vet is his best friend, and you should
not try to diagnose your pet's illness by yourself.

SOME CANINE DISEASES

Amateur diagnosis is dangerous because the symptoms of so many dog diseases
are alike, but you should be familiar with most of the diseases which can strike
your dog.

COUGHS, COLDS, BRONCHITIS, PNEUMONIA

Respiratory diseases may affect the dog because he is forced to live in a
human rather than a natural doggy environment. Being subjected to a draft
or cold after a bath, sleeping near an air conditioner or in the path of air from
a fan or near a hot air register or radiator can cause one of these respiratory
ailments. The symptoms are similar to those in humans. However, the germs
of these diseases are different and do not affect both dogs and humans so that
they cannot catch them from each other. Treatment is pretty much the same as

for a child with the same illness. Keep the puppy warm, quiet, well fed. Your veterinarian has antibiotics and other remedies to help the pup fight back.

If your puppy gets wet, dry him immediately to guard against chilling. Wipe his stomach after he has walked through damp grass. Don't make the common mistake of running your dog to the vet every time he sneezes. If he seems to have a light cold, give him about a quarter of an aspirin tablet and see that he doesn't overexercise.

MAJOR DISEASES OF THE DOG

With the proper series of inoculations, your Irish Setter will be almost completely protected against the following canine diseases. However, it occasionally happens that the shot doesn't take and sometimes a different form of the virus appears, against which your dog may not be protected.

Rabies: This is an acute disease of the dog's central nervous system and is spread by the bite of an infected animal, the saliva carrying the infection. Rabies occurs in two forms. The first is "Furious Rabies" in which the dog shows a period of melancholy or depression, then irritation, and finally paralysis. The first period lasts from a few hours to several days. During this time the dog is cross and will try to hide from members of the family. He appears restless and will change his position often. He loses his appetite for food and begins to lick, bite and swallow foreign objects. During the "irritation" phase the dog is spasmodically wild and has impulses to run away. He acts in a fearless manner and runs and bites at everything in sight. If he is caged or confined he will fight at the bars, often breaking teeth or fracturing his jaw. His bark becomes a peculiar howl. In the final or paralysis stage, the animal's lower jaw becomes paralyzed and hangs down; he walks with a stagger and saliva drips from his mouth. Within four to eight days after the onset of paralysis, the dog dies.

The second form of rabies, "Dumb Rabies," is characterized by the dog's walking in a bear-like manner with his head down. The lower jaw is paralyzed and the dog is unable to bite. Outwardly it may seem as though he has a bone caught in his throat.

Even if your pet should be bitten by a rabid dog or other animal, he can probably be saved if you get him to the vet in time for a series of injections. However, by the time the symptoms appear the disease is so far advanced that no cure is possible. But remember that an annual rabies inoculation is almost certain protection against rabies.

Distemper: Young dogs are most susceptible to distemper, although it may affect dogs of all ages. The dog will lose his appetite, seem depressed, chilled, and run a fever. Often he will have a watery discharge from his eyes and nose. Unless treated promptly, the disease goes into advanced stages with infections of the lungs, intestines and nervous system, and dogs that recover may be left with some impairment such as a twitch or other nervous mannerism. The best protection against this is very early inoculation—preferably even before the puppy is old enough to go out into the street and meet other dogs.

Hepatitis: Veterinarians report an increase in the spread of this virus disease in recent years, usually with younger dogs as the victims. The initial symptoms—drowsiness, vomiting, great thirst, loss of appetite and a high temperature—closely resemble distemper. These symptoms are often accompanied by swellings on the head, neck and lower parts of the belly. The disease strikes quickly and death may occur in a few hours. Protection is afforded by injection with a new vaccine.

Leptospirosis: This disease is caused by bacteria which live in stagnant or slow-moving water. It is carried by rats and dogs, and many dogs are believed to get it from licking the urine or feces of infected rats. The symptoms are increased thirst, depression and weakness. In the acute stage, there is vomiting, diarrhea and a brown discoloration of the jaws, tongue and teeth, caused by an inflammation of the kidneys. This disease can be cured if caught in time, but it is best to ward it off with a vaccine which your vet can administer along with the distemper shots.

External Parasites: The dog that is groomed regularly and provided with clean sleeping quarters should not be troubled with fleas, ticks or lice. However, it would be a wise precaution to spray his sleeping quarters occasionally with an anti-parasite powder that you can get at your pet shop or from your vet. If the dog is out of doors during the tick season he should be treated with a dip-bath.

Skin Ailments: Any persistent scratching may indicate an irritation, and whenever you groom your dog, look for the reddish spots that may indicate eczema or some rash or fungus infection. Do not treat him yourself. Take him to the veterinarian as some of the conditions may be difficult to eradicate and can cause permanent harm to his coat.

FIRST AID FOR YOUR DOG

In general, a dog will lick his cuts and wounds and they'll heal. If he swallows anything harmful, chances are he'll throw it up. But it will probably make you feel better to help him if he's hurt, so treat his wounds as you would your own. Wash out the dirt and apply an antiseptic or ointment. If you put on a bandage, you'll have to do something to keep the dog from trying to remove it. A large cardboard ruff around his neck will prevent him from licking his chest or body. You can tape up his nails to keep him from scratching, or make a "bootie" for his paws.

If you think your dog has a broken bone, before moving him apply a splint just as you would to a person's limb. If there is bleeding that won't stop, apply a tourniquet between the wound and heart, but loosen it every few minutes to prevent damage to the circulatory system.

If you are afraid that your dog has swallowed poison and you can't get the vet fast enough, try to induce vomiting by giving him a strong solution of salt water or mustard in water.

SOME "BUTS"

First, don't be frightened by the number of diseases a dog can get. The majority of dogs never get any of them. If you need assurance, look at any book on human diseases. How many have you had?

Don't become a dog-hypochondriac. Veterinarians have enough work taking care of sick dogs and doing preventive work with their patients. Don't rush your pet to the vet every time he sneezes or seems tired. All dogs have days on which they feel lazy and want to lie around doing nothing.

THE FEMALE PUPPY

If you want to spay your female you can have it done while she is still a puppy. Her first seasonal period will probably occur between eight and ten months, although it may be as early as six or delayed until she is a year old. She may be spayed before or after this, or you may breed her (at a later season) and still spay her afterward.

The first sign of the female's being in season is a thin red discharge, which will increase for about a week, when it changes color to a thin yellowish stain, lasting about another week. Simultaneously there is a swelling of the vulva, the dog's external sexual organ. The second week is the crucial period, when she could be bred if you wanted her to have puppies, but it is possible for the period to be shorter or longer, so it is best not to take unnecessary risks at any time. After a third week the swelling decreases and the period is over for about six months.

If you have an absolutely climb-proof and dig-proof run within your yard, it will be safe to leave her there, but otherwise the female in season should be shut indoors. Don't leave her out alone for even a minute; she should be exercised only on leash. If you want to prevent the neighborhood dogs from hanging around your doorstep, as they inevitably will as soon as they discover that your female is in season, take her some distance away from the house before you let her relieve herself. Take her in the car to a nearby park or field for a chance to stretch her legs. After the three weeks are up you can let her out as before, with no worry that she can have puppies until the next season. But if you want to have her spayed, consult your veterinarian about the time and age at which he prefers to do it. With a young dog the operation is simple and after a night or two at the animal hospital she can be at home, wearing only a small bandage as a souvenir.

GROOMING YOUR IRISH SETTER

The flat, straight coat of the Irish Setter has a tendency to snarl and become matted. A daily grooming with a stiff brush will smooth it out and will preserve the rich sheen. Frequent brushings will also guard against a doggy odor.

Teach him to jump up on a low platform or bench for his grooming. While he will probably keep himself clean for the most part, you will have a really sleek-looking dog if you allow 10 or 15 minutes a day for a grooming session. At your pet shop or kennel purchase a grooming brush with fairly stiff bristles. When you brush your dog, brush down toward his back, and do it vigorously. The purpose of the brushing is not just to improve his appearance but to remove dirt from the hairs and skin and any dead hairs. At the same time you may brush away flea eggs and other parasites. During the summer months examine him carefully for any ticks that may be adhering to his skin. If you find ticks,

Like this girl, you will want to keep your Irish Setter's coat sleek by brushing him for ten or fifteen minutes every day. However, brushing will be easier and less tiring for you and the dog if he stands on a low platform or bench.

you must be sure to remove the entire insects. You can touch them with a drop of iodine or a lighted cigarette (be careful not to burn the dog) to break their grip. Then lift them off, one at a time, with a pair of tweezers or a tissue and burn them or drop them into kerosene or gasoline to kill them.

BATHING YOUR DOG

Many clean-odored, shiny-coated Irish Setters have never had a bath. Unless your dog gets into something that just must be washed out of his coat, there is little reason to bathe him. The Saturday night bath is an institution that was never meant to apply to the dog. Frequent bathing will ruin his coat and dry out his skin. If you do feel the need to bathe your dog, use one of the dog soaps with a high oil content. Wash toward the tail so any parasites may be removed. As a precaution, put some cotton into his ears and a few drops of castor oil into his eyes before bathing, to protect them from soap. Rinse him thoroughly with clear water to remove all traces of soap and dry him very

Left: To remove snarls from your Setter's long ears, use a metal comb. His coat will tend to become easily tangled and matted, so he will need daily grooming. He'll not only look better; he'll feel better too.

Below: This Irish is being rubbed down with a mitt, especially designed to bring out the highlights in his coat. Notice how the "beautician" holds the dog to keep him standing still.

Above: If fleas or other parasites plague your Setter, spray him with one of the many triple-action germicide - fungicide - antiseptics. However, make sure your dog does not lick off much of the spray.

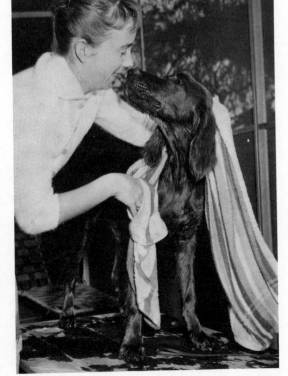

Right: "I still love you —even if you did give me a bath." Do not wash your dog unless he gets into something that can't be removed otherwise. If it is absolutely necessary to bathe him, be very careful to dry him thoroughly and follow up with a brisk rub-down.

25

carefully. Wrap him in an old towel or use an electric hair dryer and—especially in winter—keep him indoors and out of drafts until he is thoroughly dry.

There are several dry baths on the market that will do a good cleaning job on your dog and will deter or kill fleas or other parasites. You might want to check with your vet before using any of these, as some dogs may develop an allergic reaction to certain chemicals.

A GROOMING TRICK

When preparing an Irish Setter for the show ring, some groomers rub their hands over the dog's coat. The oil from the palm of the human hand imparts a bright sheen to the Irish's coat.

WATCH THE TOENAILS

Many dogs that run on gravel or pavements keep their toenails down, so they seldom need clipping, But a dog that doesn't do much running, or runs on grass, will grow long toenails that can be harmful. The long nails will force the dog's toes into the air and spread his feet wide. In addition, the nails may force the dog into an unnatural stance that may produce lameness.

You can control your dog's toenails by cutting them with a special dog clipper or by filing them. Many dogs object to the clipping and it takes some experience to learn just how to do it without cutting into the blood vessels. Your vet will probably examine your dog's nails whenever you bring him in and will trim them at no extra charge. He can show you how to do it yourself in the future. If you prefer, you can file the points off your dog's nails every few weeks with a flat wooden file.

If you use clippers for your dog's pedicure first have your vet show you how to use them. Most owners prefer to keep their dogs' nails down by filing every few weeks with a special wooden file. This method is easier and safer than clipping.

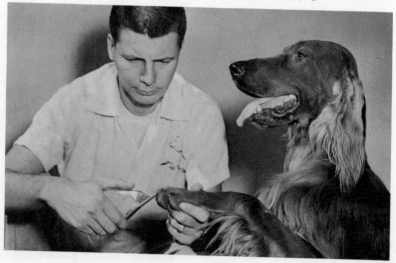

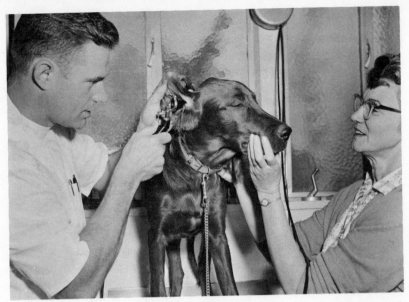

If your Setter often scratches his ears or shakes his head, his ears probably should be checked for accumulations of wax or more serious irritations. You can treat fly bites yourself, but ear mites and infections require a visit to the vet. Notice the patient attitude of the dog.

CHECK THE EARS AND TEETH

If your Irish Setter scratches at his ears or shakes his head, probe his ears very cautiously with a cotton swab dipped in mineral or castor oil. You may find an accumulation of wax that will work itself out. Any signs of dirt or dried blood in the ears probably indicates ear mites or an infection and requires treatment by your vet. In the summer, especially when flies are heavy, the dog may have sore ears from fly bites. If that happens, wash his ears with warm water and a mild soap, cover with a mild ointment and try to keep him indoors until his ears have healed.

If you give your Irish Setter a hard chewing bone—the kind you can buy at a pet store—it will serve him as your toothbrush serves you and will prevent the accumulation of tartar on his teeth. However, check his mouth occasionally and take him to the vet if you find collected tartar or bloody spots on his gums.

EXERCISE

Your Irish Setter will adapt himself to your way of life. If you lead a quiet life with no exercise, so will your dog, but it won't be healthy for him. In fact, it may shorten his life. If you have a fenced-in yard where he can run around, fine. If not, long walks, even on a lead, will serve just as well. Remember that a long walk for your Irish Setter means at least a mile, not just once around the block.

4. Housebreaking and Training Your Irish Setter

The first months of your puppy's life will be a busy time. While he's getting his preventive shots and becoming acquainted with his new family, he should learn the elements of housebreaking that will make him a welcome addition to your home and community.

HOUSEBREAKING THE IRISH SETTER PUPPY

Housebreaking the puppy isn't difficult because his natural instinct is to keep the place where he sleeps and plays clean. The most important factor is to keep him confined to a fairly small area during the training period. You will find it almost impossible to housebreak a puppy who is given free run of the house. After months of yelling and screaming, you may finally get it through his head that the parlor rug is "verboten," but it will be a long, arduous process.

FIRST, PAPER TRAINING

Spread papers over the puppy's living area. Then watch him carefully. When you notice him starting to whimper, sniff the floor or run around in agitated little circles, rush him to the place that you want to serve as his "toilet" and hold him there till he does his business. Then praise him lavishly. When you removed the soiled papers, leave a small damp piece so that the puppy's sense of smell will lead him back there next time. If he makes a mistake, wash it immediately with warm water, followed by a rinse with water and vinegar. That will kill the odor and prevent discoloration.

It shouldn't take more than a few days for the puppy to get the idea of using newspaper. When he becomes fairly consistent, reduce the area of paper to a few sheets in a corner. As soon as you think he has the idea fixed in his mind, you can let him roam around the house a bit, but keep an eye on him. It might be best to keep him on leash the first few days so you can rush him back to his paper at any signs of an approaching accident.

The normally healthy puppy will want to relieve himself when he wakes up in the morning. after each feeding and after strenuous exercise. During early puppyhood any excitement, such as the return home of a member of the family or the approach of a visitor, may result in floor-wetting, but that phase should pass in a few weeks.

OUTDOOR HOUSEBREAKING

Keep in mind during the housebreaking process that you can't expect

Paper training is the first step in housebreaking. With the firm but gentle direction this pup is receiving he'll soon get the idea and will use the newspaper regularly.

too much from your puppy until he is about 5 months old. Before that, his muscles and digestive system just aren't under his control. However, you can begin outdoor training even while you are paper training the puppy. (He should have learned to walk on lead at this point. See page 38.) First thing in the morning, take him outdoors (to the curb if you are in a city) and walk him back and forth in a small area until he relieves himself. He will probably make a puddle and then just walk around uncertain of what is expected of him. You can try standing him over a piece of newspaper which may give him the idea. Some dog trainers use glycerine suppositories at this point for fast action. Praise the dog every time taking him outside brings results and he'll get the idea. After each meal take him to the same spot.

Use some training word to help your puppy learn. Pick a word that you won't use for any other command and repeat it while you are walking your dog in his outdoor "business" area. It will be a big help when the dog is older if you have some word of command that he can connect with approval to relieve himself in a strange place. You'll find, when you begin the outdoor training, that the male puppy usually requires a longer walk than the female. Both male and female puppies will squat. It isn't until he's quite a bit older that the male dog will begin to lift his leg.

NIGHTTIME TRAINING

If you hate to give up any sleep, you can train your Irish Setter puppy to go outdoors during the day and use the paper at night for the first few months. After he's older, he'll be able to contain himself all night and wait for his first

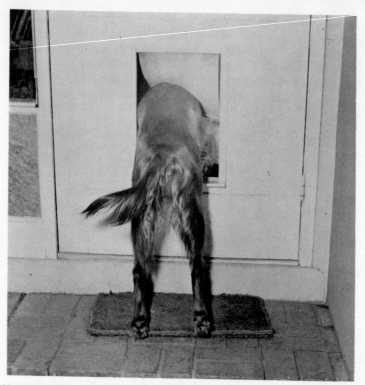

Older dogs can be trained to let themselves out when they need to relieve themselves. This swinging door opening is a great convenience—both for the dog and for his owners. He can let himself back in the house.

morning walk. However, if you want to speed up the outdoor training so that you can leave the dog alone in the house with less fear of an accident, attach his leash at night so that he has enough room to move around in his bed but not enough to get any distance away from it. When he has to go, he'll whine loudly enough to attract your attention. Then take him or let him out. You may have to get up once or twice a night for a few weeks but then you can be fairly sure that your puppy will behave indoors—although accidents will happen. Sometimes even a grown dog will suddenly—and for no apparent reason—soil the house, usually the most expensive carpet in it.

Occasionally a puppy that seems to have been housebroken will revert to indiscriminate acts all over the place. If that happens it may be necessary to go back to the beginning and repeat the paper training.

WHEN HE MISBEHAVES

Rubbing a puppy's nose in his dirt or whacking him with a newspaper may make you feel better, but it won't help train the puppy. A dog naturally *wants* to do the right thing for his master. Your job is to show him what you want. If an accident happens, ignore it unless you can catch him immediately and then in a firm tone express your displeasure and take him to the spot he should have used. When he does use the right place, be lavish with praise and petting, but first be sure he has finished. Many a puppy has left a trail of water across a floor because someone interrupted him to tell him how well he was doing.

PUPPY DISCIPLINE

A 6- or 8-week-old puppy is old enough to understand what is probably the most important word in his vocabulary—"NO!" The first time you see the puppy doing something he shouldn't do, chewing something he shouldn't chew or wandering in a forbidden area, it's time to teach him. Shout "No" and stamp your foot, hit the table with a piece of newspaper or make some other loud noise. Dogs, especially very young ones, don't like loud noises and your misbehaving pet will readily connect the word with something unpleasant. If he persists, repeat the "No," hold him firmly and slap him sharply across the nose. Before you protest to the A.S.P.C.A. you should realize that a dog does not resent being disciplined if he is doing something wrong and is caught in the act. However, do not chase a puppy around while waving a rolled-up newspaper at him or trying to swat him. Punish him only when you have a firm hold on him. Above all, never call him to you and then punish him. He must learn to associate coming to you with something pleasant.

Teach your Irish Setter to stay away from cars by discouraging him with a firm "No." If he persists in car-chasing, ask a friend to shoot a water pistol at him from the car as you drive past.

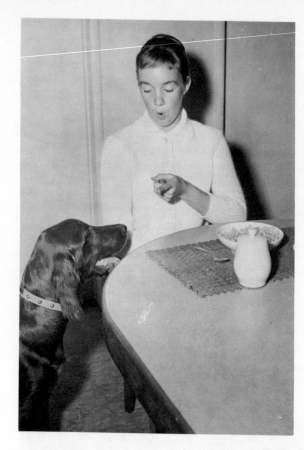

Begging for food may at first seem cute and appealing, but a dog who is allowed to do it habitually may eventually become a nuisance to both you and your guests. A well-disciplined dog should not be permitted to hang around the table and "mooch" tidbits.

Every puppy will pick things up. So the second command should be "Drop it!" or "Let go!" Don't engage in a tug-of-war with the puppy, but take the forbidden object from him even if you have to pry his jaws open with your fingers. Many dogs will release what they are holding if you just blow sharply into their faces. Let your dog know that you are displeased when he picks up something he shouldn't.

If you give him toys of his own, he will be less likely to chew your possessions. Avoid soft rubber toys that he can chew to pieces. A firm rubber ball or a tennis ball or a strong piece of leather is a good plaything. Don't give him cloth toys, either, as he'll probably swallow pieces and have trouble getting them out of his system. Skip the temptation to give him an old slipper, because it will be hard for him to distinguish between that and a brand-new pair you certainly won't want him to chew.

However, even with training, reconcile yourself to the fact that during puppy-hood things will be chewed and damaged, but that's a passing phase in the growth of the dog.

Give your pup some hard rubber toys. He likes to feel that they are "his," and will be much less tempted to chew up such irresistible items as your slippers.

JUMPING ON PEOPLE

A dog that likes people shows his affection for the human race by jumping on them. That may be cute when it's done by a tiny dog, but a full-grown Irish Setter that jumps up on your friends can be just a bit of a social hazard. The cure is fairly simple if you act to nip this habit early. When your dog jumps on people, ask them to lift their knees and send him flying back. After a few lessons of that type, he'll develop a more restrained greeting. Another method is to grab the dog's front paws and flip him backward.

Everyone knows that chairs are more comfortable than the floor, but climbing on furniture is as serious a breach of canine etiquette as begging at the table. This Setter seems to know he's out of line, and soon will learn to keep all fours firmly on the floor.

CLIMBING ON FURNITURE

If your Irish Setter shows a fondness for climbing on furniture, this is another habit you'll have to break early. The upholstery holds the scent of the people he likes, and besides, it's more comfortable than the hard floor or even the carpet. Sometimes verbal corrections will be enough to establish the fact that the furniture is taboo. If not, try putting crinkly cellophane on the furniture to keep him off. If that doesn't work, you can get liquids at your pet store that you can't smell, but whose odor keeps the dog off.

5. Obedience Training for Your Irish Setter

The purpose of obedience training is not to turn your dog into a puppet but to make him a civilized member of the community in which he will live, and to keep him safe. This training is most important as it makes the difference between having an undisciplined animal in the house or having an enjoyable companion. Both you and your dog will learn a lot from training.

HOW A DOG LEARNS

The dog is the one domestic animal that seems to want to do what his master asks. Unlike other animals that learn by fear or rewards, the dog will work willingly if he is given a kind word or a show of affection.

The hardest part of dog training is communication. If you can get across to the dog what you want him to do, he'll do it. Always remember that your dog does not understand the English language. He can, however, interpret your tone of voice and your gestures. By associating certain words with the act that accompanies them, the dog can acquire a fairly large working vocabulary. Keep in mind that it is the sound rather than the meaning of the words that the dog understands. When he doesn't respond properly, let him know by the tone of your voice that you are disappointed, but follow each correction with a show of affection.

YOUR PART IN TRAINING

You must patiently demonstrate to your dog what each simple word of command means. Guide him with your hands and the training leash through whatever routine you are teaching him. Repeat the word associated with the act. Demonstrate again and again to give the dog the chance to make the connection in his mind. (In psychological language, you are conditioning him to give a specific response to a specific stimulus.)

Once he begins to get the idea, use the word of command without any physical guidance. Drill him. When he makes mistakes, correct him, kindly at first, more severely as his training progresses. Try not to lose your patience or become irritated, and never slap him with your hand or the leash during a training session. Withholding praise or rebuking him will make him feel badly enough.

When he does what you want, praise him lavishly with words and with pats. Don't rely on dog candy or treats in training. The dog that gets into the habit of performing for treats will seldom be fully dependable when he can't smell or see one in the offing. When he carries out a command, even though his

Raising a pup is much like raising a child. Both learn quickly when treated with a combination of gentleness and firmness. Both need to be handled with patience, and should be praised lavishly when they obey or respond quickly to training.

performance is slow or sloppy, praise him and he will perform more readily the next time.

THE TRAINING VOICE

When you start training your Irish Setter, use your training voice, giving commands in a firm, clear tone. Once you give the command, persist until it is obeyed even if you have to pull the dog protestingly to obey you. He must learn that training is different from playing, that a command once given must be obeyed no matter what distractions are present. Remember that the tone and sound of your voice, not loudness, are the qualities that will influence your dog.

Be consistent in the use of words during training. Confine your commands to as few words as possible and never change them. It is best for only one

Like children, Irish Setters naturally want to please others. It is up to you to bring out the best qualities in both through intelligent care. This little boy understands that his dog loves affection as much as he does.

person to carry on the dog's training because different people will use different words and tactics that will confuse the animal. The dog who hears "come," "get over here," "hurry up," "here, Rover," and other commands when he is wanted will become totally confused.

TAKE IT EASY

Training is hard on the dog—and on the trainer. A young dog just cannot take more than 10 minutes of training at a stretch, so limit the length of your first lessons. You'll find that you, too, will tend to become impatient when you stretch out a training session, and losing your temper won't help either of you. Before and after each lesson have a play period, but don't play during a training session. Even the youngest dog soon learns that schooling is a serious matter; fun comes afterward.

Don't spend too much time on one phase of training or the dog will become bored. And always try to end a training session on a pleasant note. If the dog doesn't seem to be getting what you are trying to show him, go back to something simpler that he can do. This way you will end every lesson with a pleasant feeling of accomplishment. Actually, in nine cases out of ten, if your dog isn't doing what you want, it's because you're not getting the idea over to him properly.

WALKING ON LEAD

"Doggy" people call the leash a "lead," so we'll use that term here. With your Irish Setter, don't go in for any kind of fancy lead or collar. The best lead for training purposes is the 6-foot webbed-cloth lead, usually olive-drab in color.

As for the collar, you'll need a metal-link collar called a "choke" collar. Even though the name may sound frightening, it won't hurt your dog and it's an absolute *must* in training. It tightens when you snap the lead, eases when you relax your grip. It's important to put the collar on properly. Slide

Don't be alarmed by its name; the "choke" collar won't hurt your dog. Pass the ring end of the chain over his neck. This metal-link collar is an absolute · training necessity.

Disgruntled? Well, that's only natural until the dog gets used to a collar and lead. You can let him roam with a light leather collar and a dangling lead, but it isn't safe to let your dog wander freely while wearing a choke collar.

the chain around your dog's neck so that you can attach the lead to the ring at the end of the chain which passes *over*, not under, his neck.

Put the collar and lead on the puppy and let him walk around the house first with the lead dragging on the floor. This is just to let him get the feel of the strange object around his neck. But a word of caution for afterward: don't let the dog wander around with the choke collar on. If it's loose he'll lose it, and it's possible for it to catch on any projection and choke him. For his license tag and rabies tag you can get a light leather collar that fits more snugly.

Now, here's a lesson for you. From the start, hold the lead firmly in your right hand. Keep the dog at your left side. You can use your left hand to jerk the lead when necessary to give corrections or to bring the dog closer to you. Do not *pull* on the lead. Give it a sharp snap when you want to correct the dog, and then release it. The dog cannot learn from being pulled around. He will learn when he finds that doing certain things results in a sharp jerk; doing other things allows him to walk comfortably on lead.

At first, the puppy will fight the lead. He'll probably plant all four feet or his rear end on the ground and wait for your next move. Be patient. Short tugs on the lead will help him learn his part in walking with you. If he gets overexcited, calm him before taking off the lead and collar and picking him up. He must learn there's nothing to fear. (Incidentally, if the lesson is being given on a city street, it might be a good idea to carry some paper to clean up the mess he may leave in his excitement.)

When you begin lead training, hold the lead in your right hand and keep the dog on your left side. Use your left hand to tug at the lead when corrections are necessary.

TRAINING TO SIT

Training your dog to sit should be fairly easy. Stand him on your left side, holding the lead fairly short, and command him to "Sit." As you give the verbal command, pull up slightly with the lead and push his hindquarters down (you may have to kneel to do this). Do not let him lie down or stand up. Keep him in a sitting position for a moment, then release the pressure on the lead and praise him. Constantly repeat the command word as you hold him in a sitting position, thus fitting the word to the action in his mind. After a while, he will begin to get the idea and will sit without your having to push his back down. When he reaches that stage, insist that he sit on command. If he is slow to obey, slap his hindquarters with the end of the lead to get him down fast. Teach him to sit on command facing you as well as when he is at your side. When he begins sitting on command with the lead on, try it with the lead off.

THE "LIE DOWN"

The object of this is to get the dog to lie down either on the verbal command "Down!" or when you give him a hand signal, your hand raised, palm toward

Your İrish Setter is alert, intelligent and eager to please. It is up to you to bring out his best qualities through proper training.

A disciplined dog is always a pleasure. You can take him anywhere with you, for he is a genuine companion, never a nuisance.

the dog—a sort of threatening gesture. This is one of the most important parts of training. A well-trained dog will drop on command and stay down whatever the temptation—car-chasing, cat-chasing, or another dog across the street.

Don't start this until the dog is almost letter-perfect in sitting on command. Then, place the dog in a sit. Force him down by pulling his front feet out forward while pressing on his shoulders and repeating "Down!" Hold the dog down and stroke him gently to let him know that staying down is what you expect of him.

After he begins to get the idea, slide the lead under your left foot and give the command "Down!" At the same time, pull on the lead. This will help get the dog down. Meanwhile, raise your hand in the down signal. Don't expect to accomplish all this in one session. Be patient and work with the dog. He'll cooperate if you show him just what you expect him to do.

THE "STAY"

The next step is to train your dog to stay in either a "sit" or "down" position. Sit him at your side. Give him the command "Stay," but be careful not to use his name with that command as hearing his name may lead him to think that some action is expected of him. If he begins to move, repeat "Stay" firmly and hold him down in the sit. Constantly repeat the word "stay" to fix the meaning of that command in his mind. When he stays for a short time, gradually increase the length of his stay. The hand signal for "stay" is a downward sweep of your hand toward the dog's nose, with the palm toward him. While he is sitting, walk around him and stand in front of him. Hold the lead at first; later, drop the lead on the ground in front of him and keep him sitting. If he bolts, correct him severely and force him back to a sit in the same place.

Use some word such as "okay" or "up" to let him know when he can get up, and praise him well for a good performance. As this practice continues, walk farther and farther away from him. Later, try sitting him, giving him the command to stay, and then walk out of sight, first for a few seconds, then for longer periods. A well-trained dog should stay where you put him without moving for three minutes or more.

Similarly, practice having him stay in down position, first with you near him, later when you step out of sight.

THE "COME" ON COMMAND

A young puppy will come a-running to people, but an older puppy or dog will have other plans of his own when his master calls him. However, you can train your dog to come when you call him if you begin when he is young. At first, work with him on lead. Sit the dog, then back away the length of the lead and call him, putting as much coaxing affection in your voice as possible. Give an easy tug on the lead to get him started. When he does come, make a big fuss over him and it might help to hand him a piece of dog candy or food as a reward. He should get the idea soon. Then attach a long piece of cord to the lead—15 or 20 feet—and make him come to you from that distance. When he's coming pretty consistently, have him sit when he reaches you.

Always praise your dog generously when he comes on command. Show your affection by the tone of your voice and even by giving him an unexpected snack, perhaps a piece of dog candy.

Whether your Irish is a city pet or a working retriever, obedience training is absolutely necessary. Like people, dogs need to be civilized; they are happier when they know what you expect of them and are able to give it.

Don't be too eager to practice coming on command off lead. Wait till you are certain that you have the dog under perfect control before you try calling him when he's free. Once he gets the idea that he can disobey a command to come and get away with it, your training program will suffer a serious setback. Keep in mind that your dog's life may depend on his immediate response to a command to come when he is called. If he disobeys off lead, put the collar back on and correct him severely with jerks of the lead. He'll get the idea.

In training your dog to come, never use the command when you want to punish him. He should associate the "come" with something pleasant. If he comes very slowly, you can speed his response by pulling on the lead, calling him and running backward with him at a brisk pace.

At first, practice the "sit," "down," "stay" and "come" indoors; then try it in an outdoor area where there are distractions to show the dog that he must obey under any conditions.

HEELING

"Heeling" in dog language means having your pet walk alongside you on your left side, close to your left leg, on lead or off. With patience and effort

This trainer is perfecting the "stand." Notice the position of his hands, one under the dog's jaw, to keep the head high, the other at the tail. A dog who has mastered the "stand" will remain stationary and will not show resentment when strangers handle him.

you can train your dog to walk with you even on a crowded street or in the presence of other dogs. However, don't begin this part of his training too early. Normally, a dog much under 6 months old is just too young to absorb the idea of heeling.

Put the dog at your left side, sitting. Then say "Heel" firmly and start walking at a brisk pace. Do not pull the dog with you, but guide him by tugs on the lead. Keep some slack on the lead and use your left hand to snap the lead for a correction. Always start off with your left foot and after a while the dog will learn to watch that foot and follow it. Keep repeating "Heel" as you walk, snapping the dog back into position if he lags behind or forges ahead. If he gets out of control, reverse your course sharply and snap him along after you. Keep up a running conversation with your dog, telling him what a good fellow he is when he is heeling, letting him know when he is not.

At first limit your heeling practice to about 5 minutes at a time; later extend it to 15 minutes or a half hour. To keep your dog interested, vary the routine. Make right and left turns, change your pace from a normal walk to a fast trot to a very slow walk. Occasionally make a sharp about-face.

When teaching your dog to heel, guide, rather than pull the dog along as you walk. Move briskly, and vary your pace from time to time.

Remember to emphasize the word "heel" throughout this practice and to use your voice to let him know that you are displeased when he goes ahead or drops behind or swings wide.

If you are handling him properly, the dog should begin to get the idea of heeling in about 15 minutes. If you get no response whatever, if the dog runs away from you, fights the lead, gets you and himself tangled in the lead, it may indicate that he is still young, or that you aren't showing him what you expect him to do.

Practicing 15 minutes a day, in 6 or 7 weeks your pet should have developed to the stage where you can remove the lead and he'll heel alongside you. First try throwing the lead over your shoulder or fastening it to your belt, or remove the lead and tie a piece of thin cord (fishing line will do nicely) to his collar. Then try him off lead. Keep his attention by constantly talking; slap your left leg to keep his attention on you. If he breaks away, return to the collar and lead treatment for a while.

"HEEL" MEANS SIT, TOO

To the dog, the command "Heel" will also mean that he has to sit in heel position at your left side when you stop walking—with no additional command from you. As you practice heeling, force him to sit whenever you stop, at first using the word "Sit," then switching over to the command "Heel." He'll soon get the idea and plop his rear end down when you stop and wait for you to give the command "Heel" and start walking again.

TEACHING TO COME TO HEEL

The object of this is for you to stand still, say "Heel!" and have your dog come right over to you and sit by your left knee in heel position. If your dog has been trained to sit without command every time you stop, he's ready for this step.

Sit him in front of and facing you and step back a few feet. Say "Heel" in your most commanding tone of voice and pull the dog into heel position, making him sit. There are several different ways to do this. You can swing the dog around behind you from your right side, behind your back and to heel position. Or you can pull him toward you, keep him on your left side and swing him to heel position. Use your left heel to straighten him out if he begins to sit behind you or crookedly. This may take a little work, but the dog will get the idea if you show him just what you want.

THE "STAND"

Your Irish Setter should be trained to stand on one spot without moving his feet, and should allow a stranger to run his hands over his body and legs without showing any resentment or fear. Use the same method you used in training him to stay on the sit and down. While walking, place your left hand out, palm toward his nose, and command him to stay. His first impulse will be to sit, so be prepared to stop that by placing your hand under his body. If he's really stubborn, you may have to wrap the lead around his body near his hindquarters and hold him up until he gets the idea that this is different from the command to sit. Praise him for standing and walk to the end of the lead. Correct him strongly if he starts to move. Have a stranger approach him and run his hands over the dog's back and down his legs. Keep him standing until you come back to him. Walk around him from his left side, come to heel position, and let the dog sit as you praise him lavishly.

JUMPING EXERCISES

Most Setters love to jump, and it won't be hard to teach yours to jump over a hurdle at your command, then return to you. First let him approach the hurdle

Jumping hurdles will be fairly easy for your Setter, and he will enjoy it. It's also very good exercise. Notice how gracefully this dog takes the leap, even with a wooden dumbbell in his mouth.

and examine it. Then go back about ten feet and run toward it with the dog, holding the lead. When you reach it, shout "Over" or "Up" excitedly. Make a game of it. If the dog hestitates, it may be necessary for you to jump over it with him the first few times to give him confidence. After he jumps alone, call him and guide him back to you with the lead. After a while you can put him in sit position, facing the jump, say his name and give the command, and he will take the hurdle and return to sit in front of you. Oddly enough, a dog that is trained to jump on command will not develop the habit of jumping fences when left alone.

SIMPLE RETRIEVING

Whether or not you intend to use your Irish Setter for hunting, he should have some training in the occupation for which he was bred. It's fun to teach your dog to fetch things on command. Use a wooden dumbbell, a thick dowel stick or a thin, rolled-up magazine. While you have the dog heeling on lead, hold the object in front of him and tease him by waving it in front of his nose.

Even an Irish Setter who is not going to be used for hunting should be given some lessons in simple retrieving. If he is reluctant to give you the object, never try to force it out of his mouth. Coax him in a gentle, affectionate voice. When he lets go, reward him with pats and compliments.

Then say "Take it" and let him grab it. Walk with him while he's carrying it, and then say "Give" and take it from his mouth. If he drops it first, pick it up and "tease" him until he takes it again and holds it until you remove it.

With the dog still on lead, throw the object a few feet in front of him and encourage him to pick it up and hold it. If he won't give it up when you want it, don't have a tug-of-war. Just blow into his nostrils and he'll release his hold. Then praise him as if he had given it to you willingly.

Don't expect to accomplish all the training overnight. Generally a dog-training school will devote about 10 weeks, with one session a week, to all this training. Between lessons the dogs and their masters are expected to work about 15 minutes every day on the exercises.

If you'd like more detailed information on training your dog, you'll find it in the pages of HOW TO HOUSEBREAK AND TRAIN YOUR DOG, a Sterling-T.F.H. book.

There are dog-training classes in all parts of the country, some sponsored by the local A.S.P.C.A. A free list of dog-training clubs and schools is available from the Gaines Dog Research Center, 250 Park Avenue, New York, New York.

If you feel that you lack the time or the skill to train your dog yourself, there are professional dog trainers who will do it for you, but basically dog training is a matter of training *you* and your dog to work together as a team, and if you don't do it yourself you will miss a lot of fun.

ADVANCED TRAINING AND OBEDIENCE TRIALS

Once you begin training your Irish Setter and see how well he does, you'll probably be bitten by the "obedience bug"—the desire to enter him in obedience trials held under American Kennel Club license. Most dog shows now include obedience classes at which your dog can qualify for his "degrees" to demonstrate his usefulness as a companion dog, not merely as a pet or show dog.

The A.K.C. obedience trials are divided into three classes: Novice, Open and Utility.

In the Novice Class, the dog will be judged on the following basis:

Test	Maximum Score
Heel on leash	35
Stand for examination by judge	30
Heel free—off leash	45
Recall (come on command)	30
1-minute sit (handler in ring)	30
3-minute down (handler in ring)	30
Maximum total score	200

If the dog "qualifies" in three different shows by earning at least 50 per cent of the points for each test, with a total of at least 170 for the trial, he has earned the Companion Dog degree and the letters C.D. are entered in the stud book after his name.

After the dog has qualified as a C.D., he is eligible to enter the Open Class competition where he will be judged on this basis:

Test	Maximum Score
Heel free	40
Drop on recall	30
Retrieve (wooden dumbbell) on flat	25
Retrieve over obstacle (hurdle)	35
Broad jump	20
3-minute sit (handler out of ring)	25
5-minute down (handler out of ring)	25
Maximum total score	200

Again he must qualify in three shows for the C.D.X. (Companion Dog Excellent) title and then is eligible for the Utility Class where he can earn the Utility Dog degree in these rugged tests:

Test	Maximum Score
Scent discrimination (picking up article handled by master from group of articles)—Article 1	20
Scent discrimination—Article 2	20
Scent discrimination—Article 3	20
Seek back (picking up article dropped by handler)	30
Signal exercise (heeling, etc., on hand signal only)	35
Directed jumping (over hurdle and bar jump)	40
Group examination	35
Maximum total score	200

For more complete information about these obedience trials, write to the American Kennel Club, 221 Park Avenue South, New York 3, N.Y., and ask for their free booklet "Regulations and Standards for Obedience Trials." Spayed females and dogs that are disqualified from breed shows because of physical defects are eligible to compete in these trials.

Besides the formal A.K.C. obedience trials, there are informal "match" shows in which dogs compete for ribbons and inexpensive trophies. These shows are run by local Irish Setter clubs and by all-breed obedience clubs, and in many localities the A.S.P.C.A. and other groups conduct their own obedience shows. Your local pet shop or kennel can keep you informed about such shows in your vicinity and you will find them listed in the different dog magazines or in the pet column of your local paper.

FIELD TRAINING AND RETRIEVING

If you plan to use your Irish Setter in hunting, field training should begin fairly early in the puppy's life (concurrently with standard training procedures) so that when he is about 8 months old he will have the rudimentary knowledge of retrieving. Months of patient training are needed until your dog becomes a thoroughly obedient dog. Sometimes years pass before the two of you develop into a top-notch team. But training should begin as early as possible—perhaps at the third month—and be continued constantly.

This trainer is enticing the Setter with the object to be retrieved. Start with a rolled-up magazine, dowel stick or dumbbell; advance to a dummy, then graduate to working with a dead bird.

Young dogs—up to 10 or 12 months—should not go hunting in earnest or do much exhausting work. They tire easily, and tired dogs become slack.

The first lesson in hunting technique is fetching. Although some dogs learn almost immediately to bring back a thrown object and others take some time to get the hang of it, it doesn't seem to have a thing to do with intelligence. You can begin with the method on page 48. Another approach is to have the pup on a long cord, and when he has chased and picked up the object, reel him in like a fish. Lavish praise on him when he gets close. Eventually he'll realize that it pleases you when he brings you his training toy.

Though there are a number of good training dummies on the market, nothing compares with a small, cork-filled boat bumper. These are light and rather soft—something the pup can snatch up quickly and return with his head held high.

Getting the dog to drop a dummy in your hand requires a little patience and common sense. Again, don't get angry or engage in a tug-of-war but do be firm, prying open the dog's mouth if need be. Always praise him when he finally gives you the object. It's a good idea to let him walk around a little when he fetches something. Otherwise, he may get the idea that everything he retrieves is taken away from him immediately. (It is, but don't let him know it. Make him *want* to give it to you. An edible reward might turn the trick here.)

Never use a wounded bird when training a working retriever. This dog has brought back a dead bird which has had its wings tied together.

When the puppy has learned to retrieve one dummy, you can add another, and preferably a third, to his lessons. When you use 2 or 3 at a time, the student learns that there is often more than one bird downed. If trained with only a single dummy, he might concentrate too much on one bird and miss any others that need to be retrieved.

As the pupil is returning with a retrieved dummy, throw another one in the opposite direction so he will have to pass you to get it. As he comes back with the second dummy, fling a third in the same direction you threw the first. By throwing the objects in opposite directions, you teach the pup not to "switch birds," or shuttle between, first picking up one and then the other.

The use of multiple dummies also teaches a pup to go in the direction you point, a highly important aspect of Setter training. Urge him to cover the ground ahead of you, ranging back and forth. This is called "quartering."

Teaching this is not as difficult as it might sound. Start in an open field with the dog on a long check cord. Let him run ahead, then blow a whistle as you change your course about 90 degrees. At the noise, the pup will stop and look around to see what's going on. When you're sure he sees you, motion with your arm or "cast" in the direction you're walking. He'll probably change direction with you. If not, that's what the rope is for.

When he gets ahead of you, blow the whistle and turn back again, motioning him along. Soon he'll know that when the whistle sounds, you're changing direction—and soon he'll get used to quartering on his own.

Special care is necessary when teaching a pup not to be afraid of guns. There is no better way of making a dog gun-shy than firing for the first time right next to him. The first report should not be any closer than 500 feet (farther, if the puppy has a nervous disposition), gradually moving closer.

It takes from 5 to 10 lessons to make a dog familiar with a gun's report. He'll not *like* the noise, of course, until he learns that it might mean that a wounded bird is waiting for him—then any kind of report, even a car's backfire, really excites him.

Some sportsmen use a pheasant or duck wing in teaching a pup to carry feathery objects. However, most experts feel that this is a bad practice, since a dog may develop the habit of picking up a bird by its wing. A dead bird is better, especially a pigeon or other small bird, with the wings tied securely to the body, leaving nothing for the pup to grab except the whole bird.

An Irish Setter, particularly a young one, should never be sent to retrieve such birds as magpies and crows, for these birds are likely to bite and claw the dog. The Irish naturally fights back, and may develop the bad habit of maiming all kinds of birds.

During early training it's a good idea to have an experienced Setter along. Many dogs who have learned the rudiments alone seem to forget themselves

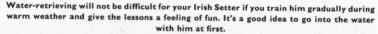

Water-retrieving will not be difficult for your Irish Setter if you train him gradually during warm weather and give the lessons a feeling of fun. It's a good idea to go into the water with him at first.

"Good show!" Whenever your dog performs well, whatever the feat, praise him lavishly.

when in the presence of other dogs. If a good Setter is around during the field training, the youngster not only accepts company, but actually picks up proper conduct by watching the older dog.

Water-retrieving lessons should begin during the warm months. When you introduce your dog to water, don't pick him up and toss him in. Let him get in gradually. Make it fun; put on your bathing suit and join him. Disregard retrieving exercises the first couple of times the pup goes swimming. The best way to introduce the student to the water is in the company of older dogs. He'll pick up good water habits from them, and pretty soon your young'un will be bounding in and out like an expert.

When teaching your dog to retrieve from the water, use either a dummy or a dead bird rather than breaking him in on a wounded duck. Chances are that he will drop a fighting bird at the water line to readjust his hold and this may develop into a habit.

"Pointing" cannot be taught, but almost all hunting dogs do so naturally. However, some, after a short point, go into the thicket after a bird. Here's another place where a check line comes in handy.

6. Caring for the Female and Raising Puppies

Whether or not you bought your female dog intending to breed her, some preparation is necessary when and if you decide to take this step.

If you are a member of the Irish Setter Club of America, you have promised to maintain quality standards and refrain from crossbreeding.

WHEN TO BREED

It is usually best to breed on the second or third season. Plan in advance the time of year which is best for you, taking into account where the puppies will be born and raised. You will keep them until they are at least 6 weeks old, and a litter of husky pups takes up considerable space by then. Other considerations are selling the puppies (Christmas vs. springtime sales), your own vacation, and time available to care for them. You'll need at least an hour a day to feed and clean up after the mother and puppies but probably it will take you much longer—with time out to admire and play with them!

CHOOSING THE STUD

You can plan to breed your female about $6\frac{1}{2}$ months after the start of her last season, although a variation of a month or two either way is not unusual. Choose the stud dog and make arrangements well in advance. If you are breeding

When breeding a female, choose a mate whose qualities will complement her weaknesses. These healthy Irish Setters, with their rich glossy coats, should produce a fine litter of pups.

for show stock, which may command better prices, a mate should be chosen with an eye to complementing the deficiencies of your female. If possible, they should have several ancestors in common within the last two or three generations, as such combinations generally "click" best. He should have a good show record or be the sire of show winners if old enough to be proven.

The owner of such a male usually charges a fee for the use of the dog. The fee varies. This does not guarantee a litter, but you generally have the right to breed your female again if she does not have puppies. In some cases the owner of the stud will agree to take a choice puppy in place of a stud fee. You should settle all details beforehand, including the possibility of a single surviving puppy, deciding the age at which he is to make his choice and take the pup, and so on.

If you want to raise a litter "just for the fun of it" and plan merely to make use of an available male Irish Setter, the most important point is temperament. Make sure the dog is friendly as well as healthy, because a bad disposition could appear in his puppies, and this is the worst of all traits in a dog destined to be a pet. In such cases a "stud fee puppy," not necessarily the choice of the litter, is the usual payment.

PREPARATION FOR BREEDING

Before you breed your female, make sure she is in good health. She should be neither too thin nor too fat. Any skin disease *must* be cured, before it can be passed on to the puppies. If she has worms she should be wormed before being bred or within three weeks afterward. It is generally considered a good idea to revaccinate her against distemper and hepatitis before the puppies are born. This will increase the immunity the puppies receive during their early, most vulnerable period.

The female will probably be ready to breed 12 days after the first colored discharge. You can usually make arrangements to board her with the owner of the male for a few days, to insure her being there at the proper time, or you can take her to be mated and bring her home the same day. If she still appears receptive she may be bred again two days later. However, some females never show signs of willingness, so it helps to have the experience of a breeder. Usually the second day after the discharge changes color is the proper time, and she may be bred for about three days following. For an additional week or so she may have some discharge and attract other dogs by her odor, but can seldom be bred.

THE FEMALE IN WHELP

You can expect the puppies nine weeks from the day of breeding, although 61 days is as common as 63. During this time the female should receive normal care and exercise. If she was overweight, don't increase her food at first; excess weight at whelping time is bad. If she is on the thin side build her up, giving some milk and biscuit at noon if she likes it. You may add one of the mineral and vitamin supplements to her food to make sure that the puppies will be healthy. As her appetite increases, feed her more. During the last two weeks the puppies grow enormously and she will probably have little room for food and less appetite. She should be tempted with meat, liver and milk, however.

As the female in whelp grows heavier, cut out violent exercise and jumping. Although a dog used to such activities will often play with the children or run around voluntarily, restrain her for her own sake.

PREPARING FOR THE PUPPIES

Prepare a whelping box a few days before the puppies are due, and allow the mother to sleep there overnight or to spend some time in it during the day to become accustomed to it. Then she is less likely to try to have her pups under the front porch or in the middle of your bed. A variety of places will serve, such as a corner of your cellar, garage, or an unused room. If the weather is warm, a large outdoor doghouse will do, well protected from rain or draft. A whelping box serves to separate mother and puppies from visitors and other distractions. The walls should be high enough to restrain the puppies, yet allow the mother to get away from the puppies after she has fed them. Four feet square is minimum size, and one-foot walls will keep the pups in until they begin to climb, when it should be built up. Then the puppies really need more room anyway, so double the space with a very low partition down the middle and you will find them naturally housebreaking themselves.

Layers of newspaper spread over the whole area will make excellent bedding and be absorbent enough to keep the surface warm and dry. They should be removed daily and replaced with another thick layer. An old quilt or washable blanket makes better footing for the nursing puppies than slippery newspaper during the first week, and is softer for the mother.

Be prepared for the actual whelping several days in advance. Usually the female will tear up papers, refuse food and generally act restless. These may be false alarms; the real test is her temperature, which will drop to below 100° about 12 hours before whelping. Take it with a rectal thermometer morning and evening, and put her in the pen, looking in on her frequently, when her temperature goes down.

WHELPING

Usually little help is needed but it is wise to stay close to make sure that the mother's lack of experience does not cause an unnecessary accident. Be ready to help when the first puppy arrives, for it could smother if she does not break the membrane enclosing it. She should start right away to lick the puppy, drying and stimulating it, but you can do it with a soft rough towel, instead. The afterbirth should follow the birth of each puppy, attached to the puppy by the long umbilical cord. Watch to make sure that each is expelled, anyway, for retaining this material can cause infection. In her instinct for cleanliness the mother will probably eat the afterbirth after biting the cord. One or two will not hurt her; they stimulate milk supply as well as labor for remaining pups. But too many can make her lose appetite for the food she needs to feed her pups and regain her strength. So remove the rest of them along with the wet newspapers and keep the pen dry and clean to relieve her anxiety.

If the mother does not bite the cord, or does it too close to the body, take over the job, to prevent an umbilical hernia. Tearing is recommended, but you can cut it, about two inches from the body, with a sawing motion of scissors,

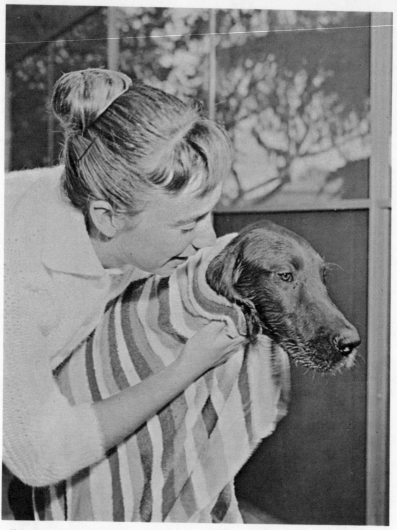

Keep a whelping female warm and comfortable. She will know what to do during birth, but it will be easier for her if she knows you are nearby, ready to assist if necessary.

sterilized in alcohol. Then dip the end in a shallow dish of iodine; the cord will dry up and fall off in a few days.

The puppies should follow each other at intervals of not more than half an hour. If more time goes past and you are sure there are still pups to come, a brisk walk outside may start labor again. If she is actively straining without producing a puppy it may be presented backward, a so-called "breech" or upside-down birth. Careful assistance with a well-soaped finger to feel for the puppy or ease it back may help, but never attempt to pull it by force against the mother. This could cause serious damage, so let an expert handle it.

If anything seems wrong, waste no time in calling your veterinarian, who can examine her and if necessary give hormones which will bring the remaining puppies. You may want his experience in whelping the litter even if all goes well. He will probably prefer to have the puppies born at his hospital rather than to get up in the middle of the night to come to your home. The mother would, no doubt, prefer to stay at home, but you can be sure she will get the best of care in his hospital. If the puppies are born at home and all goes as it should, watch the mother carefully afterward.

WEANING THE PUPPIES

Hold each puppy to a breast as soon as he is dry, for a good meal without competition. Then he may join his littermates in the basket, out of his mother's way while she is whelping. Keep a supply of evaporated milk on hand for emergencies, or later weaning. A supplementary feeding often helps weak pups over the hump. Keep track of birth weights, and take weekly readings; it will furnish an accurate record of the pups' growth and health.

After the puppies have arrived, take the mother outside for a walk and drink, and then allow her to take care of them. She will probably not want to stay away more than a minute or two for the first few weeks. Be sure to keep water available at all times, and feed her milk or broth frequently, as she needs liquids to produce milk. Encourage her to eat, with her favorite foods, until she asks for it of her own accord. She will soon develop a ravenous appetite and should have at least two large meals a day, with dry food available in addition.

Prepare a warm place to put the puppies after they are born to keep them dry and help them to a good start in life. An electric heating pad or hot water bottle covered with flannel in the bottom of a cardboard box should be set near the

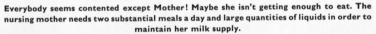

Everybody seems contented except Mother! Maybe she isn't getting enough to eat. The nursing mother needs two substantial meals a day and large quantities of liquids in order to maintain her milk supply.

mother so that she can see her puppies. She will usually allow you to help, but don't take the puppies out of sight, and let her handle things if your interference seems to make her nervous.

If the mother is normally healthy after whelping puppies and has ample milk supply for the number of puppies in the litter, it is wise to let them nurse on her until they are three to four weeks of age. If feasible, keep the mother with her puppies until they are five or six weeks of age. As long as they nurse on the mother, puppies are less vulnerable to disease.

For bottle feeding of puppies in the event of illness or death of their mother, it is wise to have an experienced breeder or veterinarian recommend the formula. Whenever possible, it is better to locate a foster mother for the puppies. The foster mother does not necessarily have to be an Irish Setter or a large breed of dog.

Be sure that all the puppies are getting enough to eat. If the mother sits or stands, instead of lying still to nurse, the probable cause is scratching from the puppies' nails. You can remedy this by clipping them, as you do hers. Manicure scissors will do for these tiny claws. Some breeders advise disposing of the smaller or weaker pups in a large litter, as the mother has trouble in handling more than six or seven. But you can help her out by preparing an extra puppy box or basket. Leave half the litter with the mother and the other half in a warm place, changing off at two-hour intervals at first. Later you may change them less frequently, leaving them all together except during the day. Try supplementary feeding, too; as soon as their eyes open, at about two weeks, they will lap from a dish, anyway.

The puppies should normally be completely weaned at five weeks, although you start to feed them at three weeks. They will find it easier to lap semi-solid food. At four weeks they will eat four meals a day, and soon do without their mother entirely. Start them on mixed dog food, or leave it with them in a dish for self-feeding. Don't leave water with them all the time; at this age everything is to play with and they will use it as a wading pool. They can drink all they need if it is offered several times a day, after meals.

As the puppies grow up the mother will go into the pen only to nurse them, first sitting up and then standing. To dry her up completely, keep the mother away for longer periods; after a few days of part-time nursing she can stay away for longer periods, and then completely. The little milk left will be reabsorbed.

AIRING THE PUPPIES

The puppies may be put outside, unless it is too cold, as soon as their eyes are open, and will benefit from the sunlight and vitamins. A rubber mat or newspapers underneath will protect them from cold or damp.

You can expect the pups to need at least one worming before they are ready to go to new homes, so take a stool sample to your veterinarian before they are three weeks old. If one puppy has worms all should be wormed. Follow the veterinarian's advice, and this applies also to vaccination. If you plan to keep a pup you will want to vaccinate him at the earliest age possible, so his littermates should be done at the same time.

7. Showing Your Irish Setter

You probably think that your Irish Setter is the best in the country and possibly in the world, but before you enter the highly competitive world of the show, get some unbiased expert opinions. Compare your dog against standards on pages 7-9. If an Irish Setter club in your vicinity is holding a match show, enter your dog and see what the judges think of him. If he places in a few match shows, then you might begin seriously considering the big-time shows. Visit a few as a spectator first and make careful mental notes of what is required of the handlers and the dogs. Watch how the experienced handlers manage their dogs to bring out their best points. See how they use pieces of liver to "bait" the dogs and keep them alert in the ring. If experts think your dog has the qualities to make a champion, you might want to hire a professional handler to show him.

ADVANCE PREPARATION

Before you go to a show your dog should be trained to gait at a trot beside you, with head up and in a straight line. In the ring you will have to gait around the edge with other dogs and then individually up and down the center runner. In addition the dog must stand for examination by the judge, who will look at him closely and feel his head and body structure. He should be taught to stand squarely, hind feet slightly back, head up on the alert. He must hold the pose when you place his feet and show animation for a piece of boiled liver in your hand or a toy mouse thrown in front of you.

Showing requires practice training sessions in advance. Get a friend to act as judge and set the dog up and "show" him for a few minutes every day.

Fortunately, the Irish Setter requires little special grooming for his show appearance if you have been conscientious about regular grooming sessions.

The day before the show, pack your kit. You will want to take a water dish and bottle of water for your dog (so that he won't be affected by a change in drinking water, and you won't have to go look for it). A chain or leash to fasten him to the bench, or stall, where he must remain during the show, and a show lead should be included, as well as grooming tools. The show lead is a thin nylon or cord collar and leash combined, which doesn't detract from the dog's appearance as much as a clumsier chain and lead. Also put in the identification ticket sent by the show superintendent, noting the time you must be there and the place where the show will be held, as well as the time of judging.

THE DAY OF THE SHOW

Don't feed your dog the morning of the show, or give him at most a light meal. He will be more comfortable in the car on the way, and will show more enthusiastically. When you arrive at the show grounds an official veterinarian will check your dog for health, and then you should find his bench and settle him there. Locate the ring where Irish Setters will be judged, take the dog to the exercise ring to relieve himself, and give him a small drink of water. After a final grooming, you have only to wait until your class is called. It is your responsibility to be at the ring at the proper time.

Then, as you step into the ring, try to keep your knees from rattling too loudly. Before you realize it you'll be out again, perhaps back with the winners for more judging and finally—with luck—it will be all over and you'll have a ribbon and an armful of silver trophies. And a very wonderful dog!

This Irish Setter is a champion. But we would know that even if we couldn't see his ribbons and trophies. His bearing and expression show the qualities of the breed, the beauty and intelligence which make the Irish sometimes a champion, always a treasured pet.